Phonics For Kids

This book belongs to:

....

CONTENTS:

Letter and sound A	Page 1
Letter and sound M	Page 5
Letter and sound T	Page 9
Letter and sound S	Page 12
Letter and sound I	Page 17
Letter and sound F	Page 21
Letter and sound D	Page 25
Letter and sound R	Page 29
Letter and sound O	Page 33
Letter and sound G	Page 37
Letter and sound L	Page 41
Letter and sound H	Page 45
Letter and sound U	Page 49
Letter and sound C	Page 53
Letter and sound B	Page 57
Letter and sound N	Page 61
Letter and sound K	Page 65
Review beginning sound	Page 69
Review beginning sound	Page 70
Letter and sound V	Page 71
Review beginning sound	Page 75
Review beginning sound	Page 76
Letter and sound E	Page 77
Letter and sound W	Page 81
Letter and sound J	Page 85
Word Search	Page 89
Sound short "a"	Page 90
Letter and sound P	Page 91
Sound short "e"	Page 95
Letter and sound Y	Page 97
Letter and sound X	Page 101
Sound short "i"	Page 103
Letter and sound Q	Page 105
Sound short "o"	Page 109
Letter and sound Z	Page 111
Sound short "u"	Page 115
Answer key	Page 117

HELLEN M. ANVIL

Join us for a gathering to celebrate a life of continuous learning.

 /helen.anvil

 /helen.anvil

 helen.m.anvil@gmail.com

LETTER A

Trace the letter **A**:

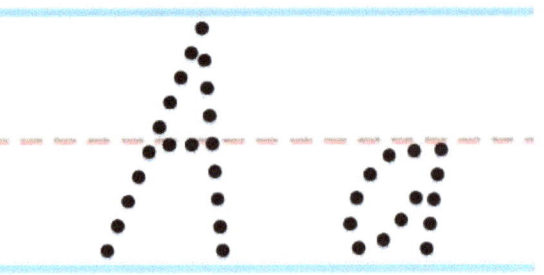

Write an upper and lower case letter **A**:

- Color all the items that begin with the **A** sound:

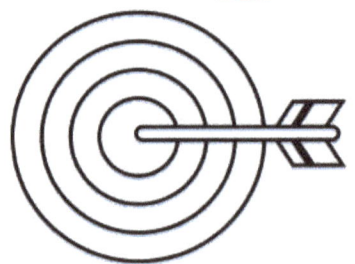
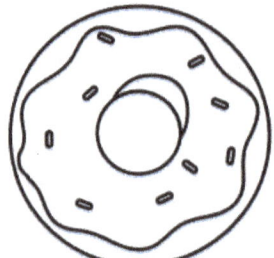

LETTER A

- Say the name of each picture. Circle each picture that begins with the **a** sound.

2

LETTER A

- Color only the squares with letter **A**.

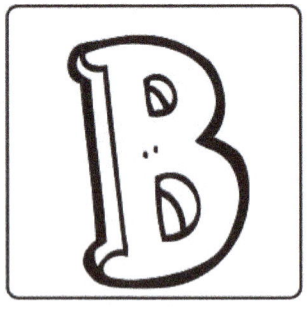 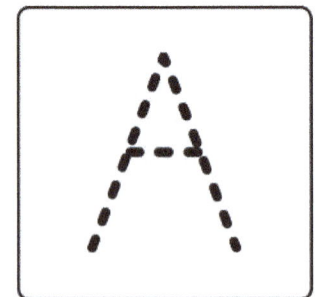 

 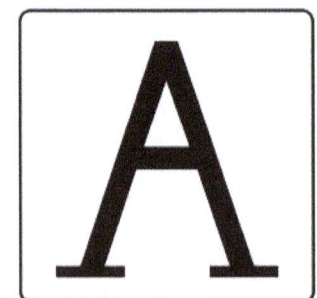 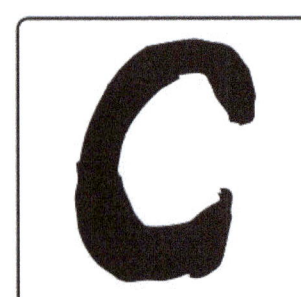

LETTER A

- Say the name of each picture. If it begins with the sound **A**, write **A a** on the line.

A a

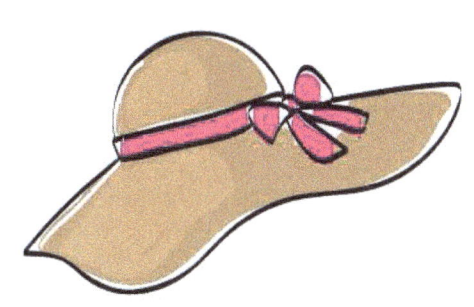

LETTER M

Trace the letter **M**:

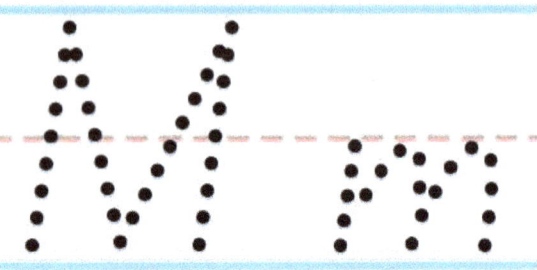

Write an upper and lower case letter **M**:

- Color all the items that begin with the **M** sound:

LETTER M

- Say the name of each picture. Draw a line from the letter **M** to each picture that begins with the **m** sound.

LETTER M

- Trace the letter **M m**. Circle the picture in each row whose name begins with the **m** sound.

LETTER M

- Complete the maze. Color the squares that have the letter **M** printed inside.

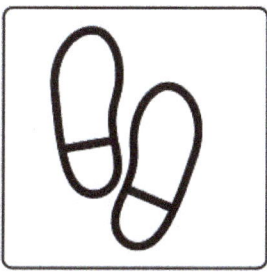  

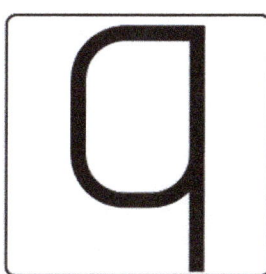  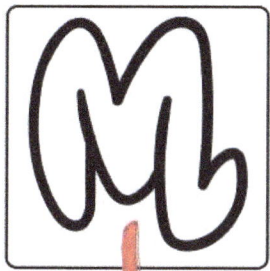

LETTER T

Trace the letter **T**:

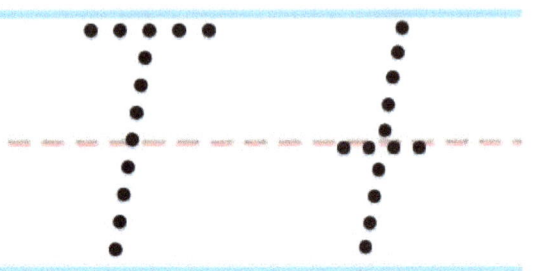

Write an upper and lower case letter **T**:

- Color all the items that begin with the letter **T**:

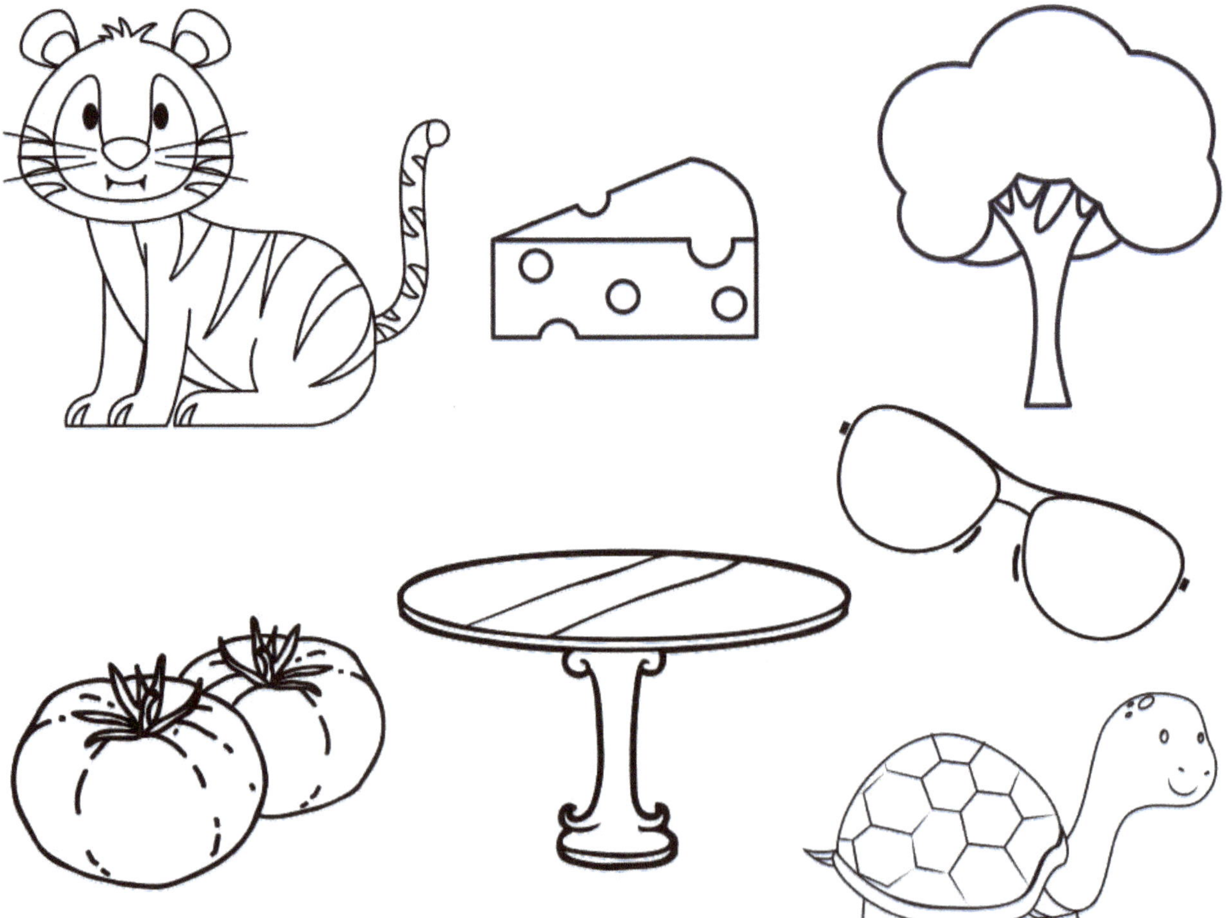

LETTER T

- Trace the letter **T t**. Circle the picture in each row whose name begins with the **t** sound.

LETTER T

- Complete the maze. Color the squares that have the letter **T** printed inside.

  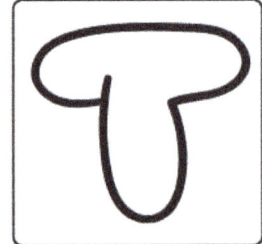

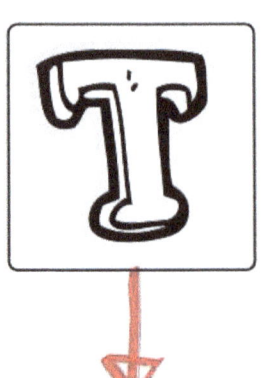 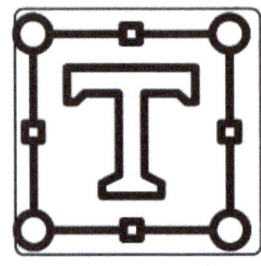 

LETTER T

- Say the name of each picture. Draw a line from the letter **T** to each picture that begins with the **t** sound.

LETTER S

Trace the letter **S**:

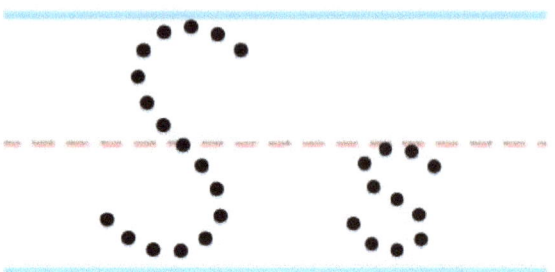

Write an upper and lower case letter **S**:

- Color all the items that begin with the letter **S**:

LETTER S

- Trace the letter **S s**. Circle the picture in each row whose name begins with the **s** sound.

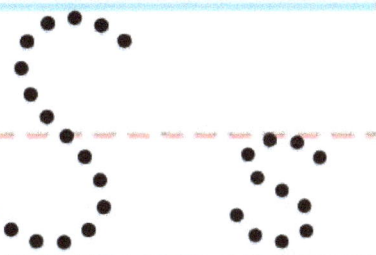   

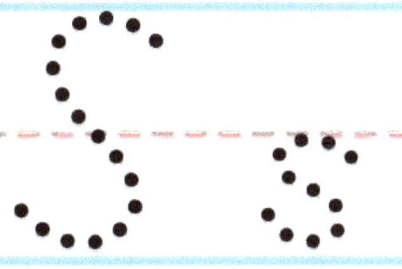   

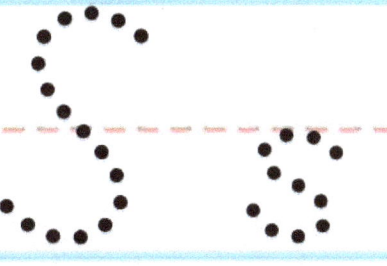   

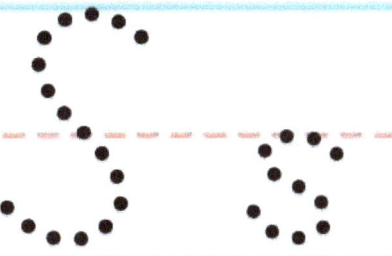   

LETTER S

- Trace the letter **S s**. Say the name of each picture. Draw a line from letter **Ss** to each picture that begins with the **s** sound.

LETTER I

Trace the letter I:

Write an upper and lower case letter I:

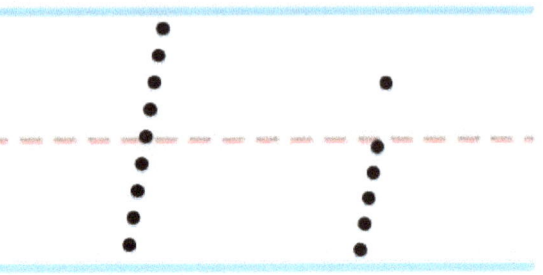

- Color all the items that begin with the letter I:

LETTER I

- Trace the letter **I i**. Circle the picture in each row whose name begins with the **i** sound.

LETTER I

- Say the name of each picture. Draw a line from letter **S** to each picture that begins with the **s** sound.

LETTER I

- Complete the maze. Color the squares that have the letter I printed inside.

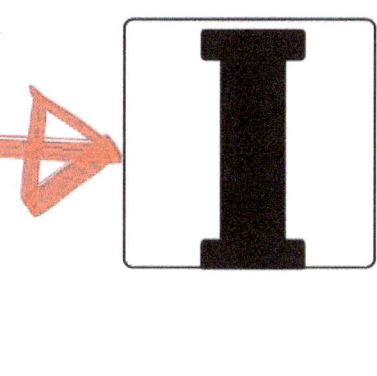

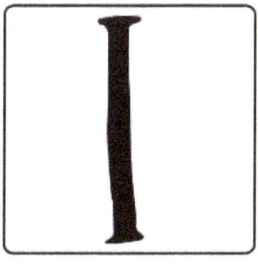

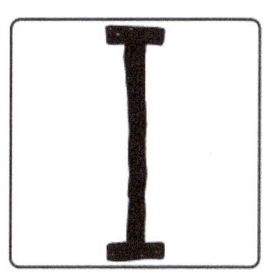

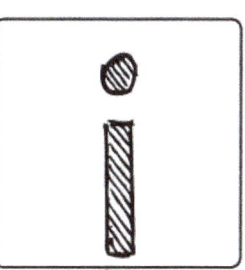

LETTER F

Trace the letter **F f**:

Write an upper and lower case letter F:

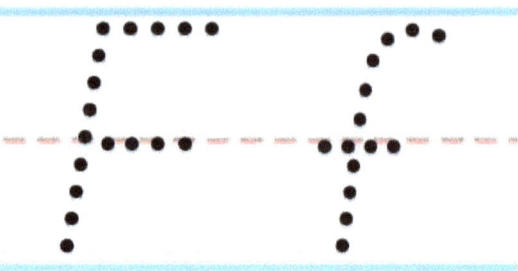

- Color all the items that begin with the letter **F**:

LETTER F

- Trace the letter **F f**. Circle the picture in each row whose name begins with the **f** sound.

LETTER F

- Say the name of each picture. Circle each picture that begins with the sound **F**:

LETTER F

- Complete the maze. Color the squares that have the letter **F** printed inside.

LETTER D

Trace the letter **D d**:

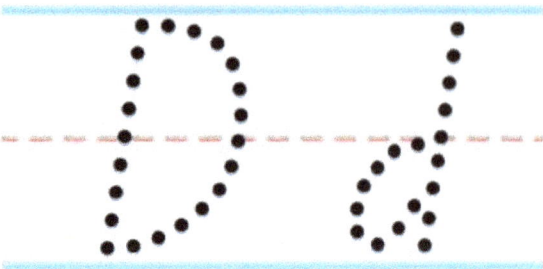

Write an upper and lower case letter **D**:

- Color all the items that begin with the letter **D**:

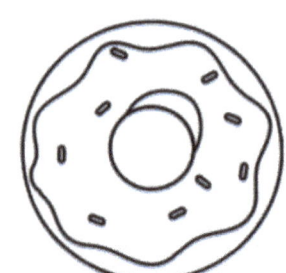

LETTER D

- Trace the letter **D d**. Circle the picture in each row whose name begins with the **d** sound.

LETTER D

- Complete the maze. Color the squares that have the letter **D** printed inside.

 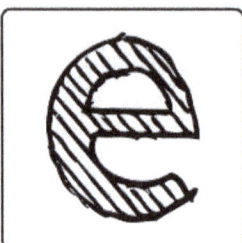 

 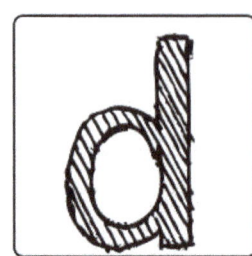 

LETTER D

- Say the name of each picture. Draw an **X** on each picture that begins with the **D** sound:

LETTER R

Trace the letter **R**:

Write an upper and lower case letter **R**:

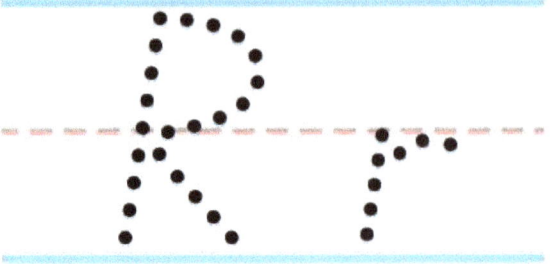

- Color all the items that begin with the **R** sound:

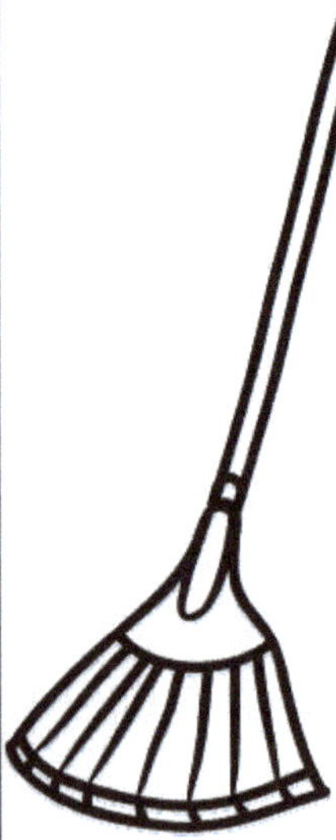

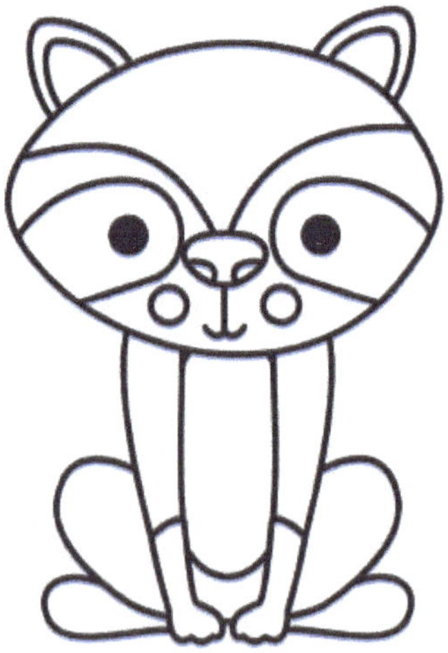

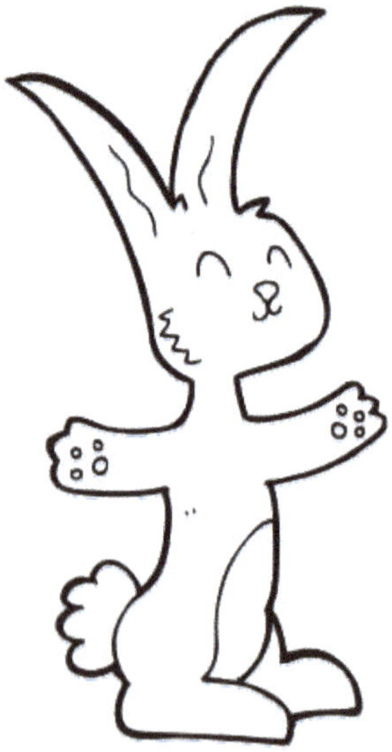

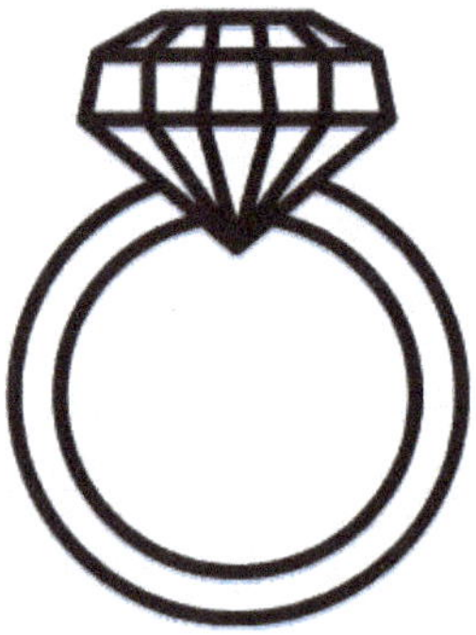

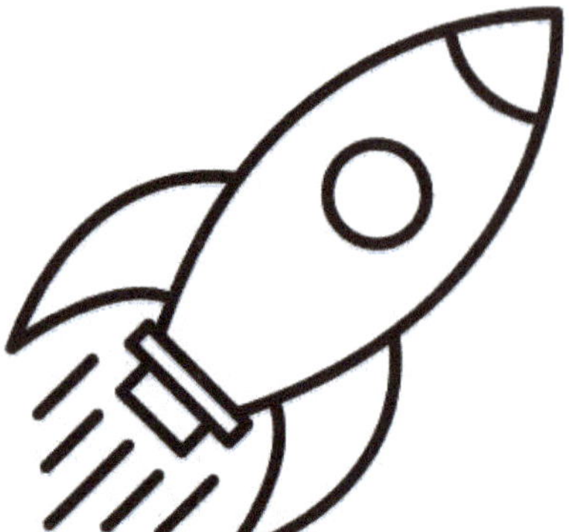

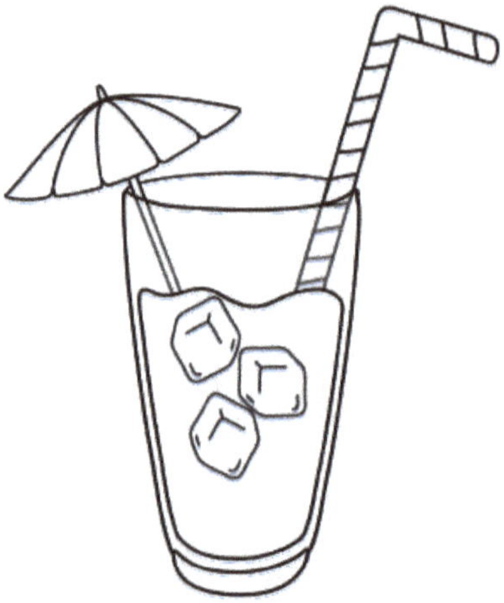

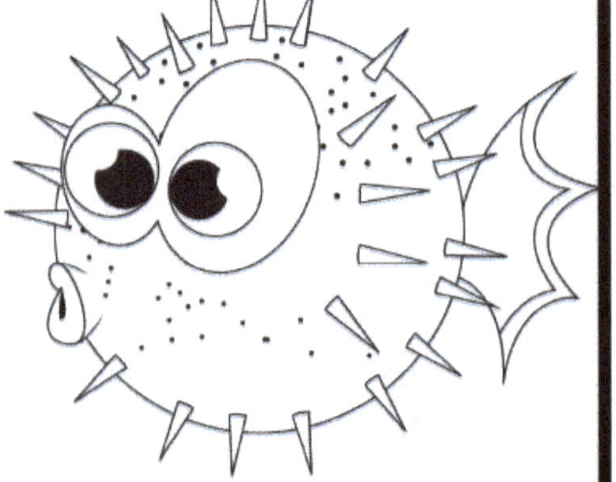

LETTER R

- Say the name of each picture. Circle each picture that begins with the **r** sound.

LETTER R

- Color only the squares with letter **R**.

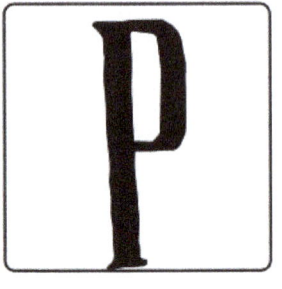  
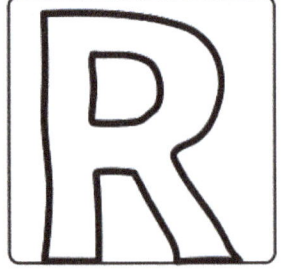  

LETTER R

- Say the name of each picture. If it begins with the sound **R**, write **R r** on the line.

LETTER O

Trace the letter O o:

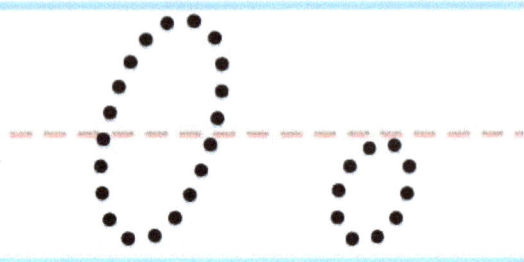

Write an upper and lower case letter O:

- Color all the items that begin with the O sound:

LETTER O

- Say the name of each picture. Draw a line from the letter O to each picture that begins with the o sound.

LETTER O

- Trace the letter O o. Circle the picture in each row whose name begins with the o sound.

LETTER O

- Say the name of each picture. Draw an **X** on each picture that begins with the **O** sound:

LETTER G

Trace the letter **G g**:

Write an upper and lower case letter **G**:

- Color all the items that begin with the letter **G**:

LETTER G

- Say the name of each picture. Circle each picture that begins with the **g** sound.

LETTER G

- Complete the maze. Color the squares that have the letter **G** printed inside.

 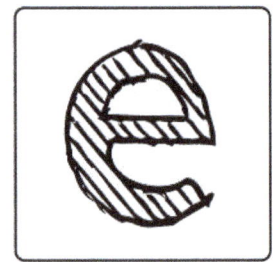 

LETTER G

- Say the name of each picture. Draw a line from the letter **G** to each picture that begins with the **g** sound.

LETTER L

Trace the letter **L l**:

Write an upper and lower case letter **L**:

- Color all the items that begin with the letter **L**:

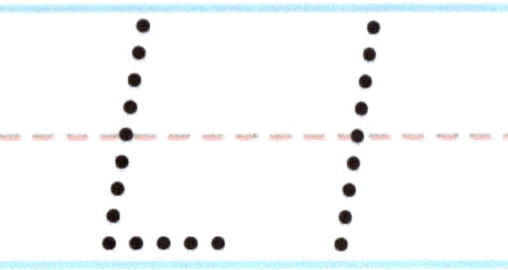

LETTER L

- Trace the letter **L l**. Circle the picture in each row whose name begins with the **l** sound.

LETTER L

- Say the name of each picture. Draw an **X** on each picture that begins with the **L** sound:

LETTER L

- Trace the letter **L l**. Say the name of each picture. Draw a line from letter **Ll** to each picture that begins with the **L** sound.

LETTER H

Trace the letter **H h**:

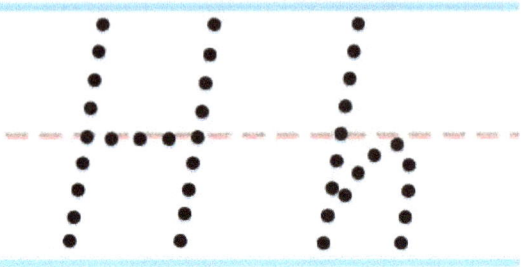

Write an upper and lower case letter **H**:

- Color all the items that begin with the letter **H**:

LETTER H

- Trace the letter **H h**. Circle the picture in each row whose name begins with the **h** sound.

LETTER H

- Say the name of each picture. Draw a line from letter **H** to each picture that begins with the **h** sound.

LETTER H

- Complete the maze. Color the squares that have the letter **H** printed inside.

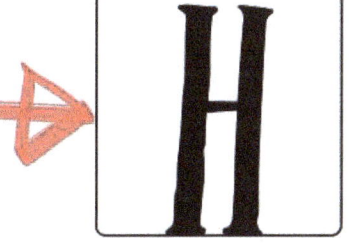  

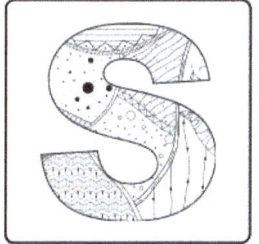  

  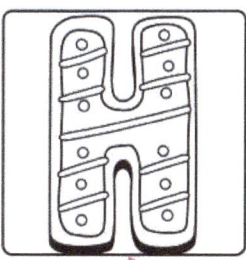

LETTER U

Trace the letter **U u**:

Write an upper and lower case letter **U**:

- Color all the items that begin with the letter **U**:

LETTER U

- Trace the letter **U u**. Circle the picture in each row whose name begins with the **U** sound.

LETTER U

- Say the name of each picture. Trace the letter **u** to complete each word.

up

unlock

uncle

under

LETTER U

- Complete the maze. Color the squares that have the letter **U** printed inside.

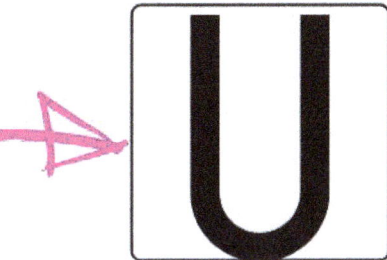  

  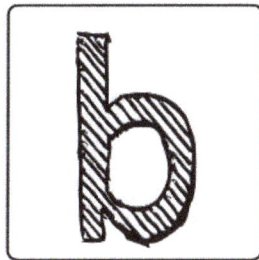

 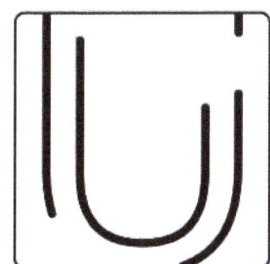 

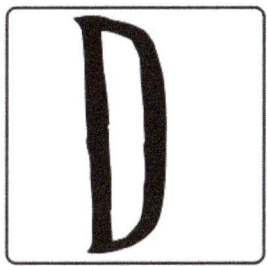 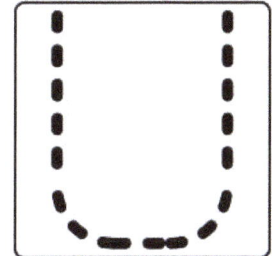 

LETTER C

Trace the letter **C c**:

Write an upper and lower case letter **C**:

- Color all the items that begin with the **C** sound:

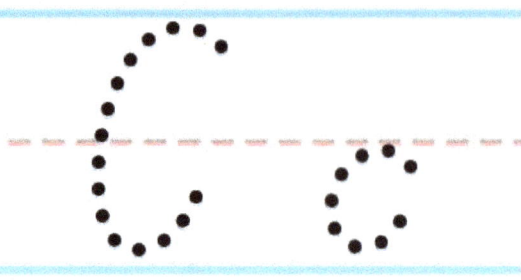

LETTER C

- Say the name of each picture. Circle each picture that begins with the **C** sound.

LETTER C

- Say the name of each picture. Trace the letter **c** to complete each word.

cat

clown

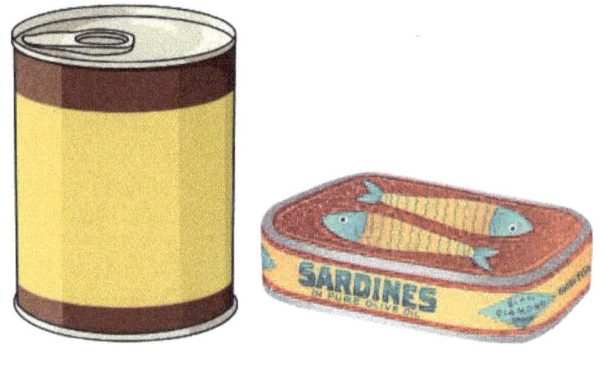

crab

can

LETTER C

- Say the name of each picture. If it begins with the sound **C**, write **C c** on the line.

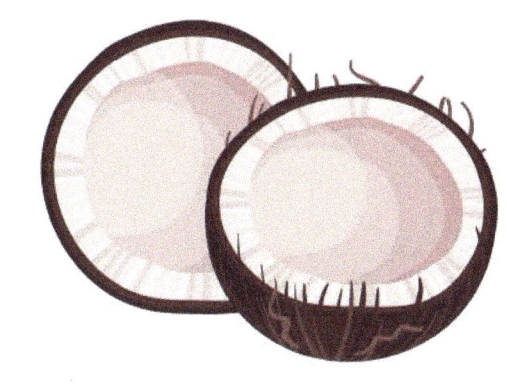

LETTER B

Trace the letter **B b**:

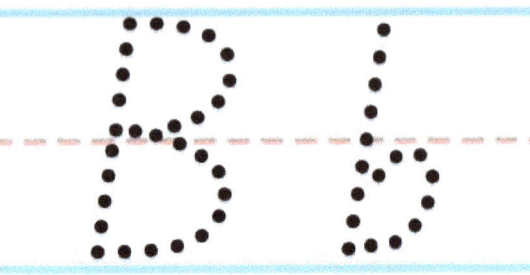

Write an upper and lower case letter **B**:

- Color all the items that begin with the **B** sound:

LETTER B

- Say the name of each picture. Draw a line from the letter **B** to each picture that begins with the **b** sound.

LETTER B

- Trace the letter **B b**. Circle the picture in each row whose name begins with the **b** sound.

LETTER B

- Complete the maze. Color the squares that have the letter **B** printed inside.

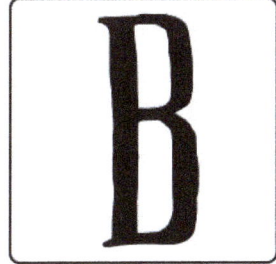  

LETTER N

Trace the letter **N n**:

Write an upper and lower case letter **N**:

- Color all the items that begin with the letter **N**:

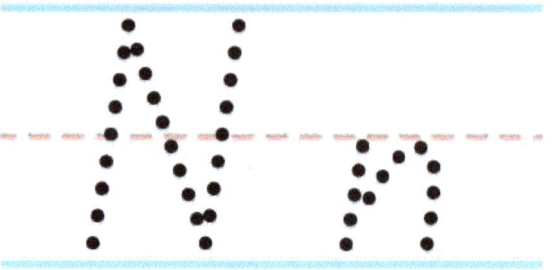

LETTER N

- Trace the letter **N n**. Circle the picture in each row whose name begins with the **n** sound.

LETTER N

- Complete the maze. Color the squares that have the letter **N** printed inside.

LETTER N

- Say the name of each picture. Draw a line from the letter **N** to each picture that begins with the **n** sound.

LETTER K

Trace the letter **K** **k**:

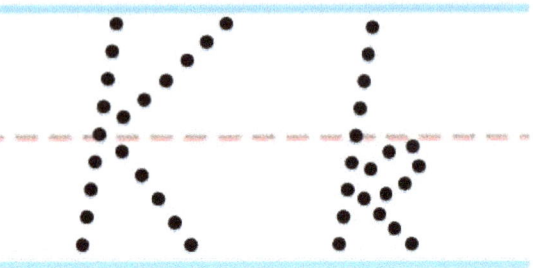

Write an upper and lower case letter **K**:

- Color all the items that begin with the letter **K**:

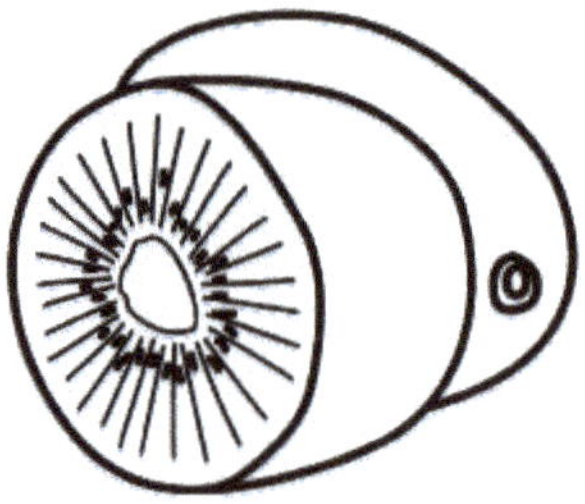

LETTER K

- Trace the letter **K k**. Circle the picture in each row whose name begins with the **k** sound.

LETTER K

- Say the name of each picture. Draw an **X** on each picture that begins with the **K** sound:

LETTER K

- Trace the letter **K k**. Say the name of each picture. Draw a line from letter **K k** to each picture that begins with the **k** sound.

- Say the name of each picture. Circle the letter of the beginning sound.

- Say the name of each picture. Circle the letter of the beginning sound.

LETTER V

Trace the letter **V v**:

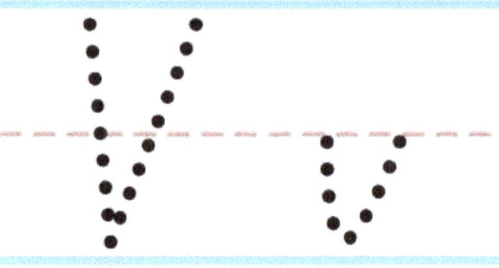

Write an upper and lower case letter **V**:

- Color all the items that begin with the letter **V**:

LETTER V

- Trace the letter **V v**. Circle the picture in each row whose name begins with the **v** sound.

LETTER V

- Say the name of each picture. Draw a line from letter **V** to each picture that begins with the **v** sound.

LETTER V

- Complete the maze. Color the squares that have the letter **V** printed inside.

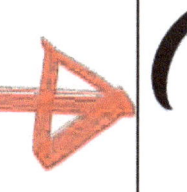

- Say the name of each picture. Circle the letter of the beginning sound.

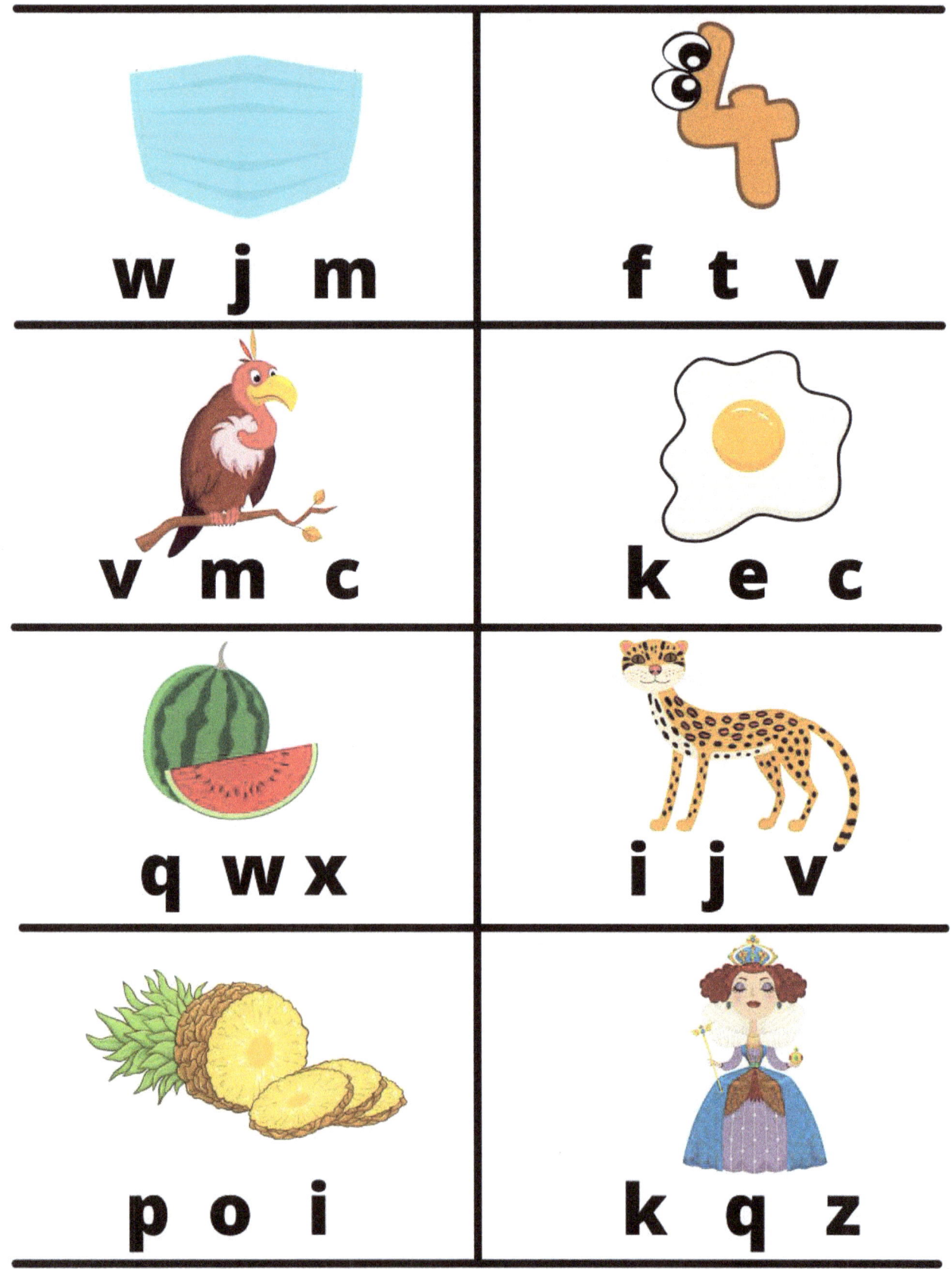

w j m

f t v

v m c

k e c

q w x

i j v

p o i

k q z

- Say the name of each picture. Circle the letter of the beginning sound.

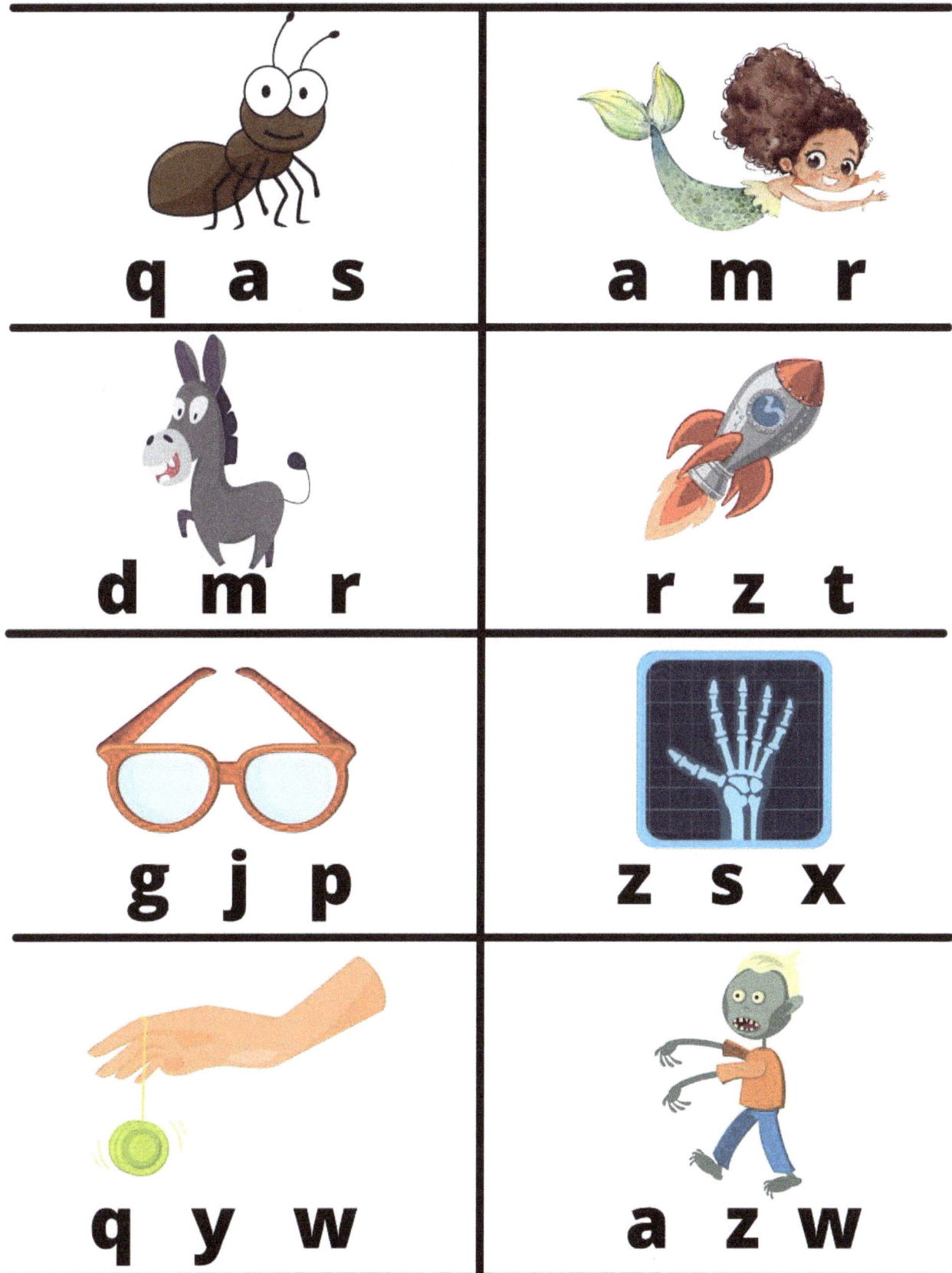

LETTER E

Trace the letter **E e**:

Write an upper and lower case letter **E**:

- Color all the items that begin with the letter **E**:

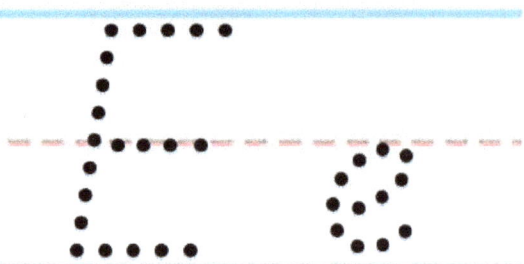

LETTER E

- Trace the letter **E e**. Circle the picture in each row whose name begins with the **e** sound.

LETTER E

- Say the name of each picture. Circle each picture that begins with the sound **E**:

LETTER E

- Complete the maze. Color the squares that have the letter **E** printed inside.

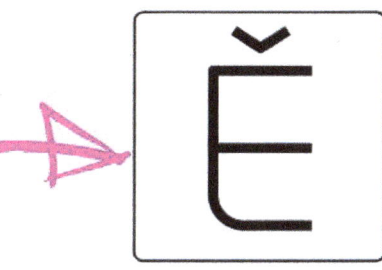  

  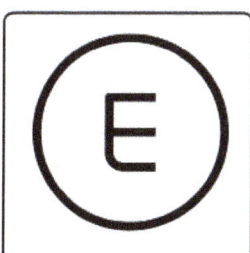

  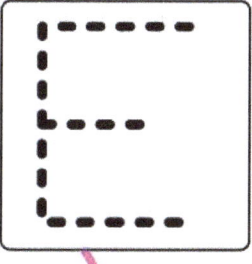

LETTER W

Trace the letter **W w**:

Write an upper and lower case letter **W**:

- Color all the items that begin with the **W** sound:

LETTER W

- Say the name of each picture. Circle each picture that begins with the **w** sound.

LETTER W

- Color only the squares with letter **W**.

LETTER W

- Say the name of each picture. If it begins with the sound **W**, write **W w** on the line.

LETTER J

Trace the letter **J j**:

Write an upper and lower case letter **J**:

- Color all the items that begin with the **J** sound:

LETTER J

- Say the name of each picture. Draw a line from the letter **J** to each picture that begins with the **j** sound.

LETTER J

- Trace the letter **J j**. Circle the picture in each row whose name begins with the **j** sound.

LETTER J

- Complete the maze. Color the squares that have the letter **J** printed inside.

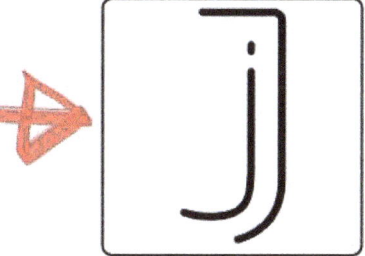 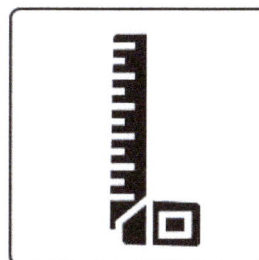 

  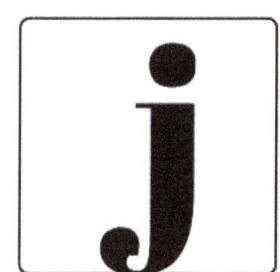

 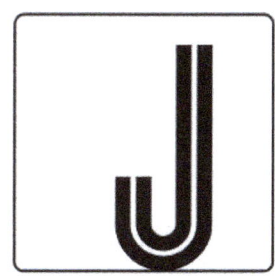 

Word search

- Can you find all the sight words in the puzzle bellow?

e	x	b	h	p	f	s	e	e
a	r	e	u	n	r	d	m	e
c	s	z	l	q	o	n	a	y
h	a	v	e	u	m	a	m	i
m	z	l	f	o	c	o	m	e
r	u	n	l	u	i	d	a	y
c	d	z	b	q	o	h	g	z
m	o	r	e	f	s	h	e	f

Word Search

each	day
are	she
more	run
from	have
see	come

short a

- Circle the word in each box that has the **short a** sound, as in **cap**.

mac	tag
map	tug
mop	tip

him	mask
hen	mist
ham	more

can	him
cob	hat
car	hot

big	beg
bag	bug
bug	bat

LETTER P

Trace the letter **P p**:

Write an upper and lower case letter **P**:

- Color all the items that begin with the letter **P**:

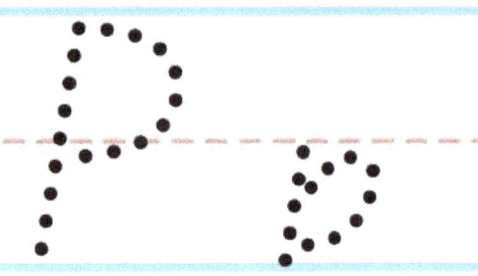

LETTER P

- Trace the letter **P p**. Circle the picture in each row whose name begins with the **p** sound.

LETTER P

- Complete the maze. Color the squares that have the letter **P** printed inside.

LETTER P

- Say the name of each picture. Draw a line from the letter **P** to each picture that begins with the **P** sound.

short e

- Say the name of each picture. Write the letter **e** to complete each **short e** word.

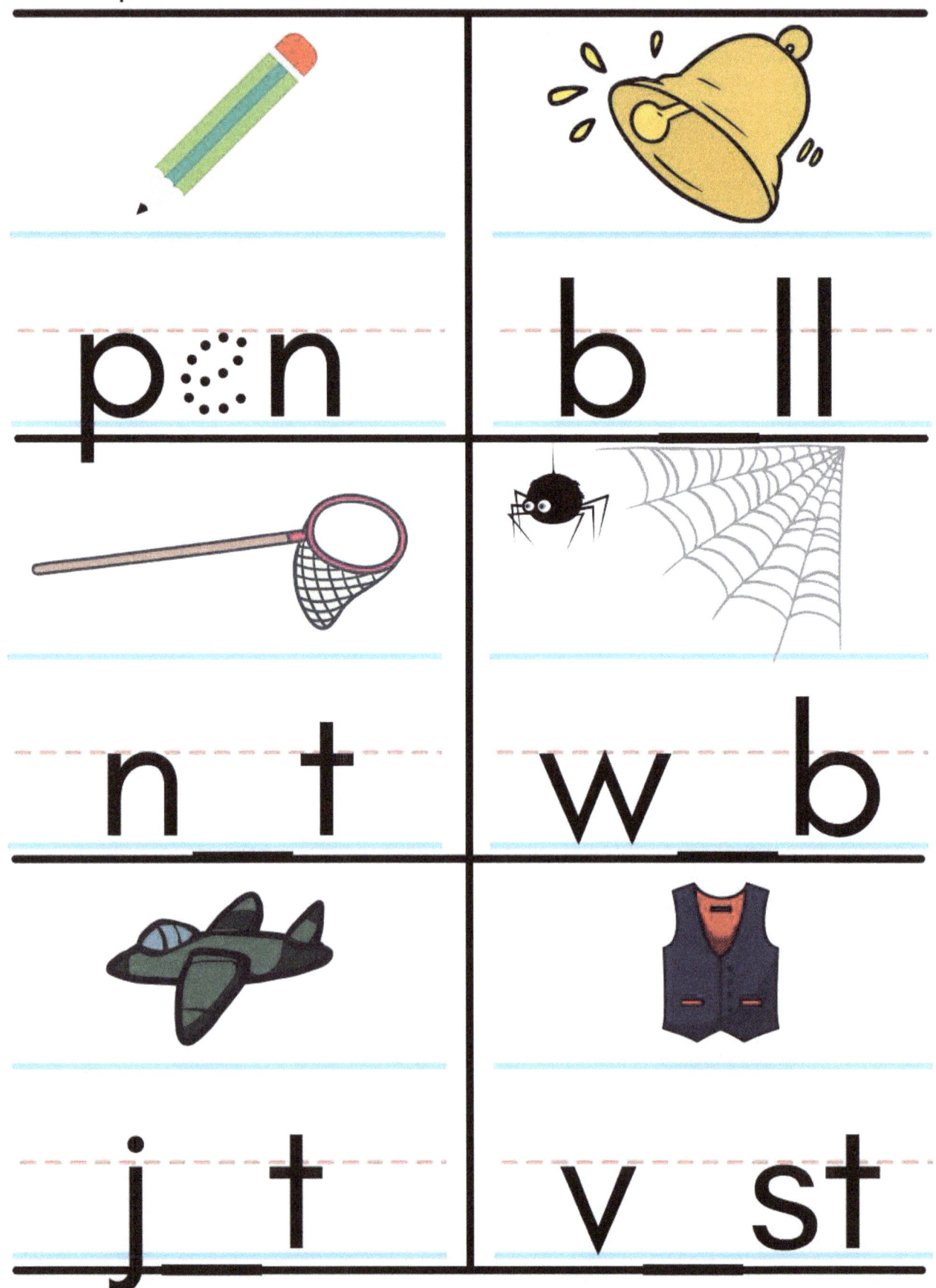

p_n   b_ll

n_t   w_b

j_t   v_st

95

short e

- Circle the word in each box that has the **short e** sound, as in **leg**.

lag / lap / **leg**	pig / **pen** / pin
ton / **ten** / tint	**dress** / drain / duck
not / nut / **net**	**tent** / tip / tint
bag / **bell** / ball	**peg** / pan / pin

96

LETTER Y

Trace the letter **Y y**:

Write an upper and lower case letter **Y**:

- Color all the items that begin with the letter **Y**:

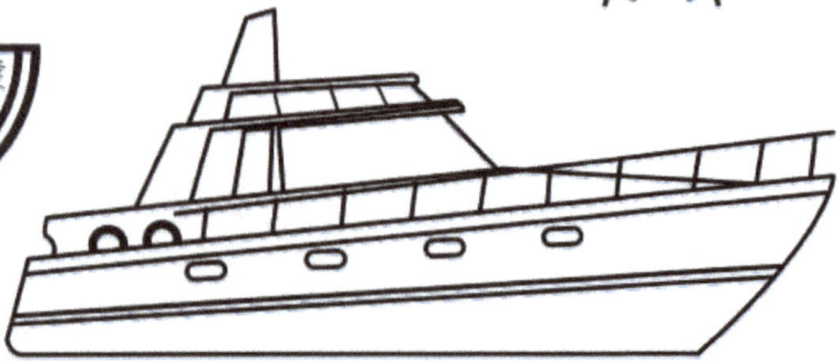

LETTER Y

- Trace the letter **Y y**. Circle the picture in each row whose name begins with the **y** sound.

LETTER Y

- Say the name of each picture. Draw an **X** on each picture that begins with the **Y** sound:

LETTER Y

- Trace the letter **Y y**. Say the name of each picture. Draw a line from letter **Y y** to each picture that begins with the **y** sound.

LETTER X

Trace the letter **X x**:

Write an upper and lower case letter **X**:

- Color all the items that begin with the letter **X**:

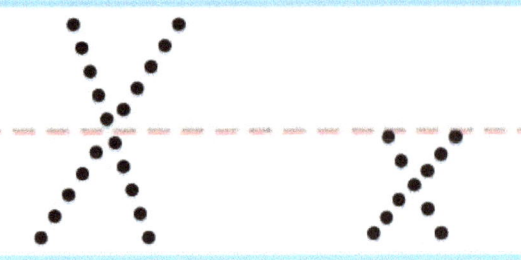
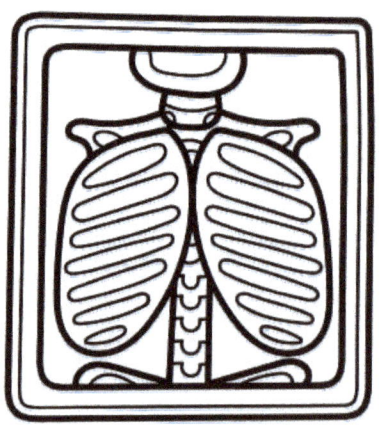

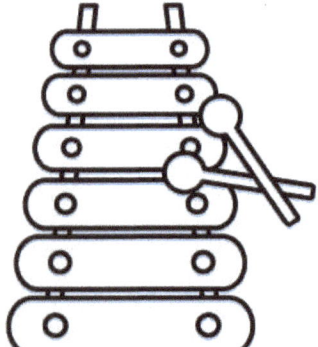

LETTER X

- Complete the maze. Color the squares that have the letter **X** printed inside.

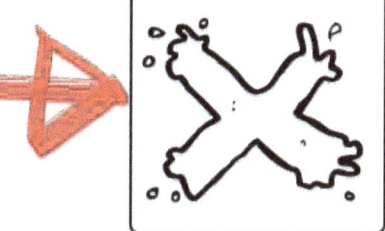  

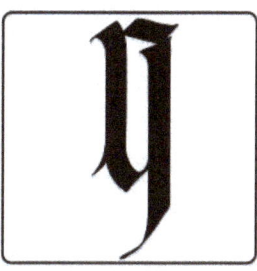  

short *i*

- Say the name of each picture. Write the letter **i** to complete each **short i** word.

short i

- Circle the word in each box that has the **short i** sound, as in **fig**.

sunk / sand / sink

wig / was / wash

sax / six / sand

fun / fan / fish

log / lips / luck

went / was / wings

bib / bell / ball

peg / pan / pin

LETTER Q

Trace the letter **Q q**:

Write an upper and lower case letter **Q**:

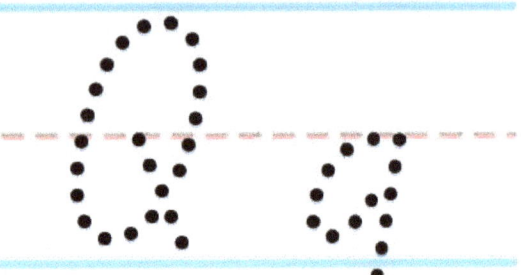

- Color all the items that begin with the letter **Q**:

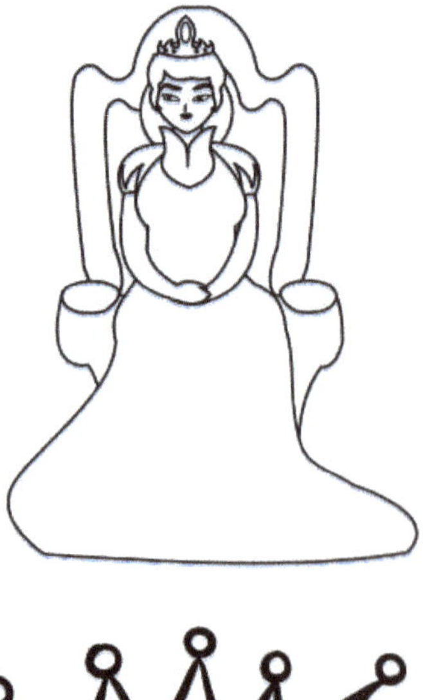

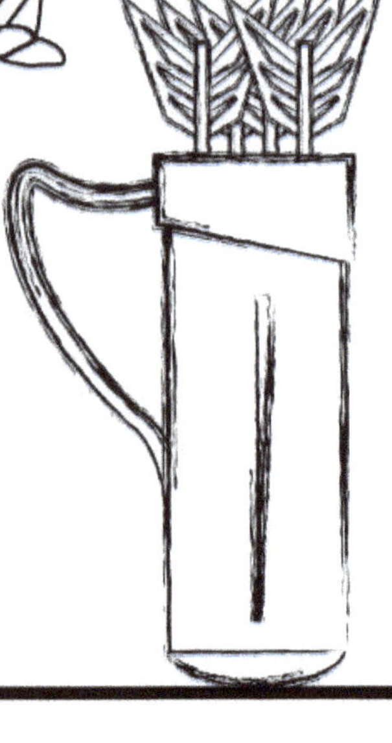

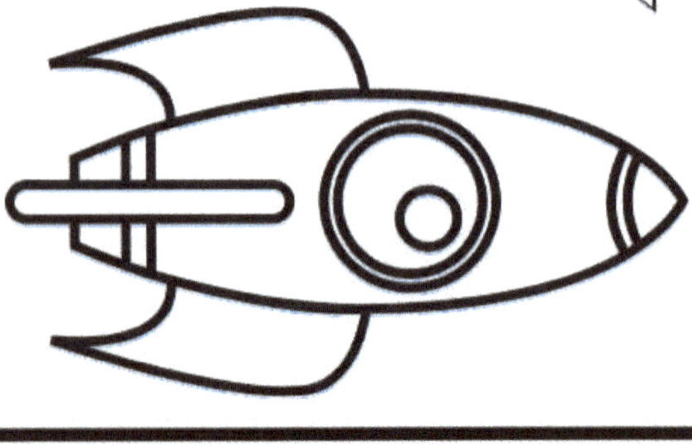

LETTER Q

- Trace the letter **Q q**. Circle the picture in each row whose name begins with the **q** sound.

LETTER Q

- Say the name of each picture. Circle each picture that begins with the sound Q:

LETTER Q

- Complete the maze. Color the squares that have the letter **Q** printed inside.

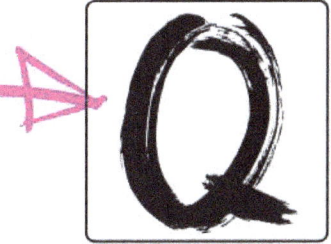  

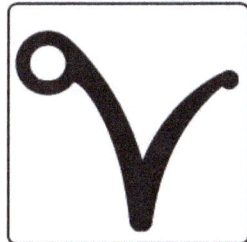  

short o

- Say the name of each picture. Write the letter **o** to complete each **short o** word.

short o

- Circle the word in each box that has the **short o** sound, as in **lock**.

log / lap / leg	dig / dog / den
tap / ten / top	doll / drain / duck
list / lock / lips	sock / sick / sack
fig / frost / frog	peg / pat / pot

LETTER Z

Trace the letter **Z z**:

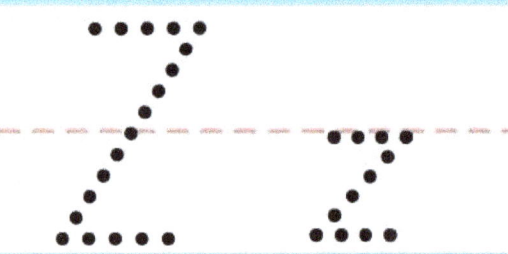

Write an upper and lower case letter **Z**:

- Color all the items that begin with the **Z** sound:

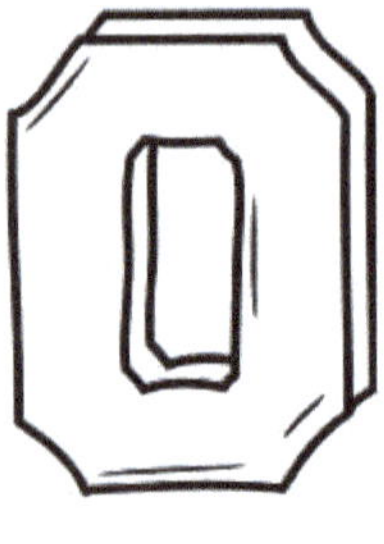

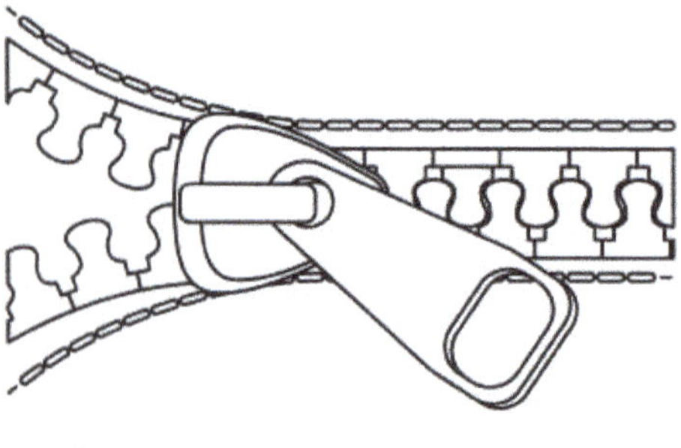

111

LETTER Z

- Say the name of each picture. Circle each picture that begins with the **Z** sound.

LETTER Z

- Say the name of each picture. Trace the letter **Z** to complete each word.

zero

zoo

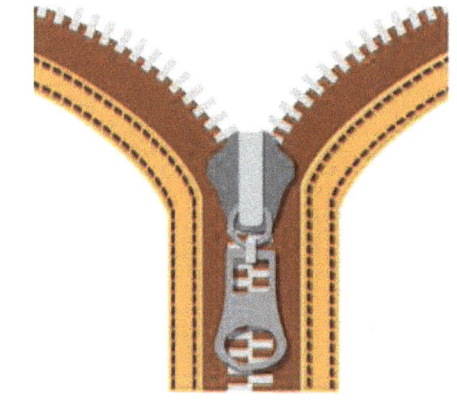

zebra

zipper

LETTER Z

- Say the name of each picture. If it begins with the sound **Z**, write **Z z** on the line.

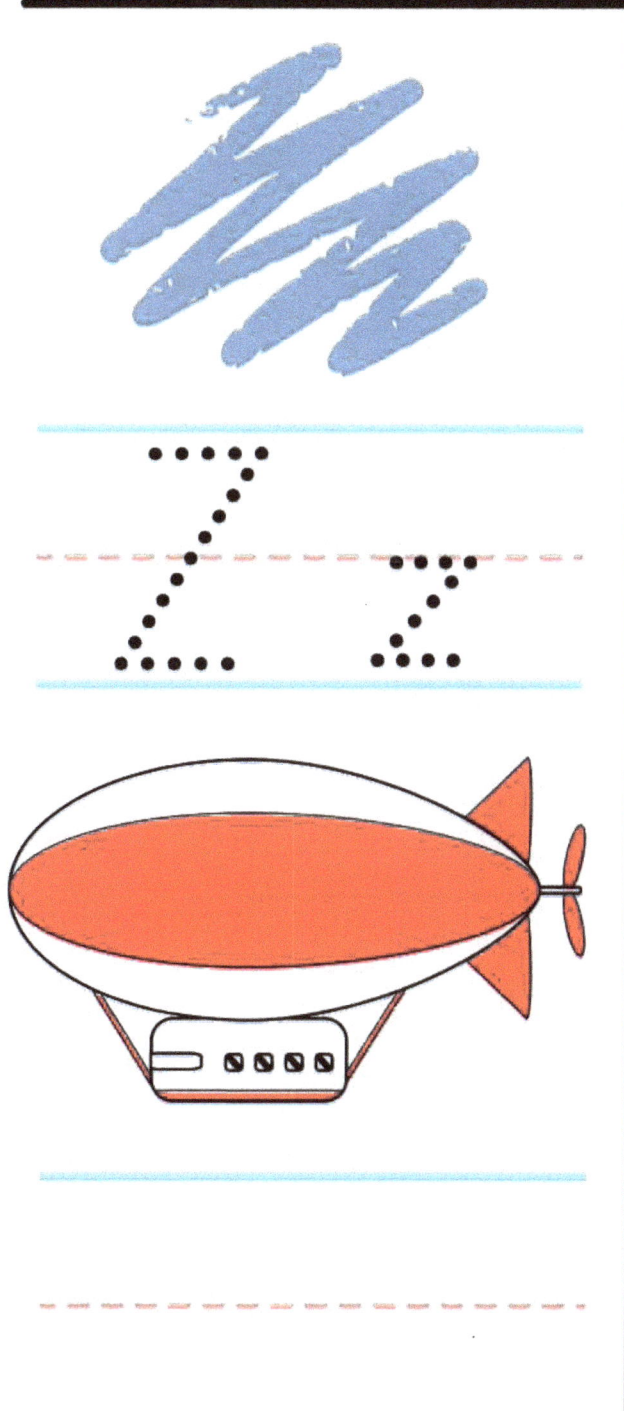

short u

- Say the name of each picture. Write the letter **u** to complete each **short u** word.

m u g   n _ t

s _ n   d _ ck

dr _ m   h _ t

short u

- Circle the word in each box that has the **short u** sound, as in **cup**.

mug / man / milk	rot / rug / ray
gap / gum / gas	doll / drain / duck
not / net / nut	sun / sick / sack
jug / jar / jet	dog / drum / dot

Answer Key

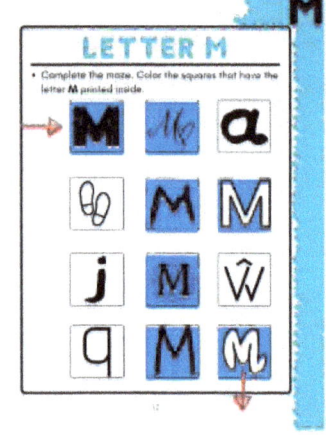
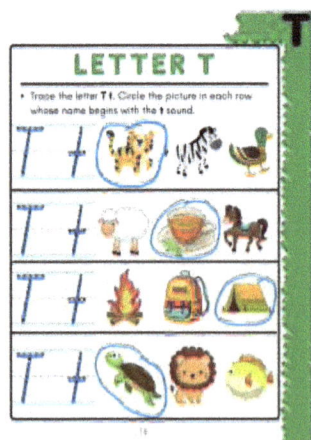

Answer Key

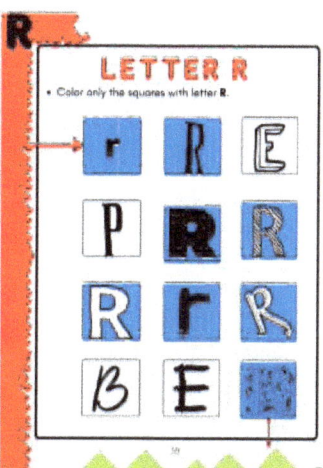

Answer Key

Answer Key

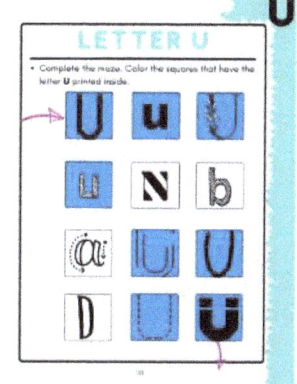

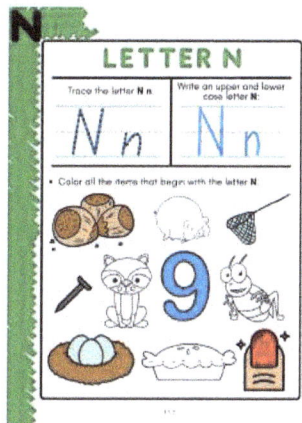
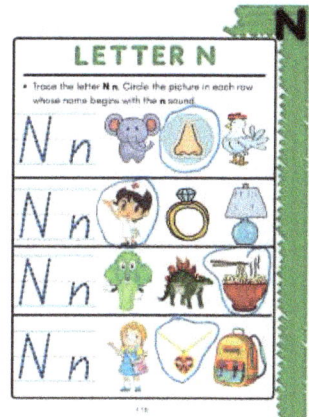

Answer Key

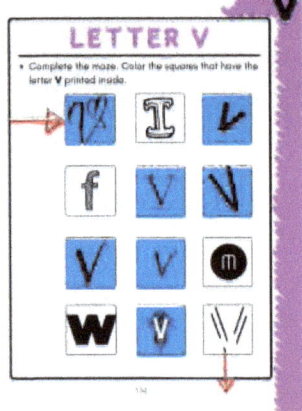
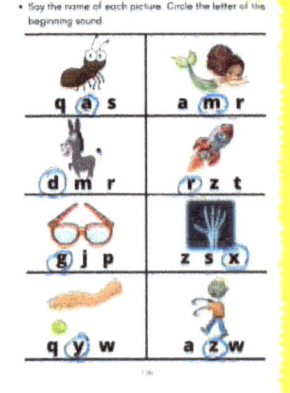

Answer Key

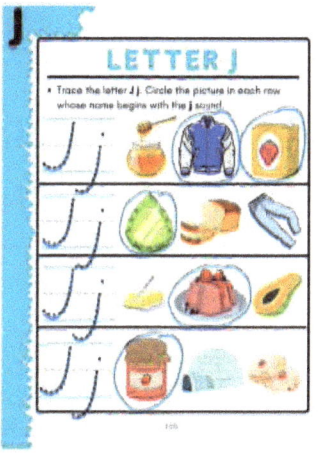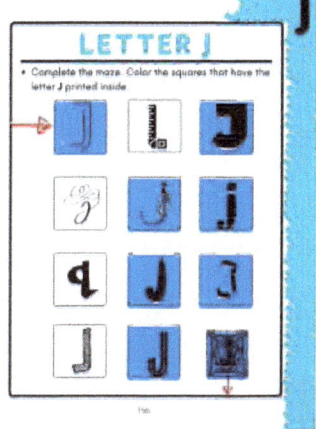
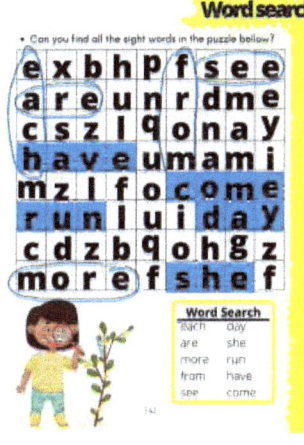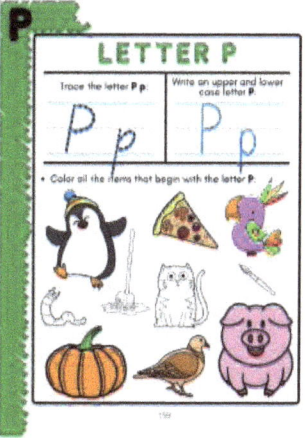

Answer Key

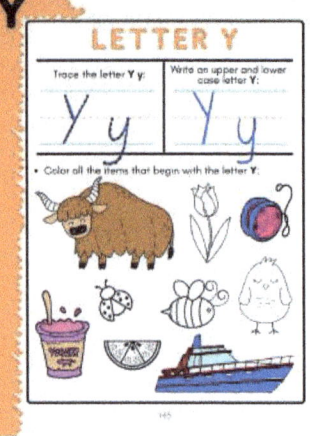

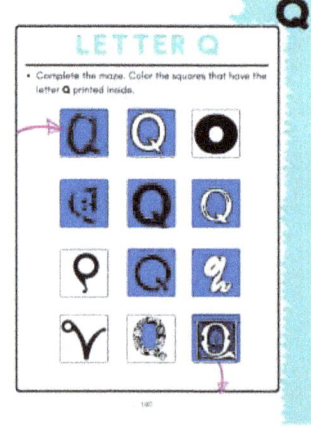

Answer Key

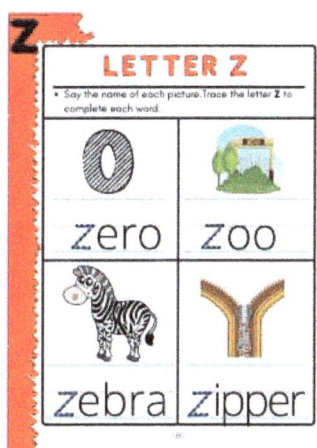

GREAT JOB!
ACHIVEMENT DIPLOMA

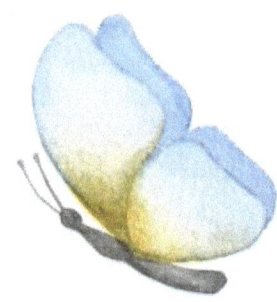

This certifies that

....

has completed all the activities in

Phonics Activity Book

You are on your way
to becoming a reader!

You are a sounds
superstar!

© Copyrights 2021 - All rights reserved

You may not reproduce, duplicate or send the contents of this book without direct written permission from the author. You cannot hereby despite any circumstance blame the publisher or hold him or her te legal responsibility for any reparation, compensation or monetary forfeiture owing to the information included herein, either in a direct or indirect way.

Legal Notice: This book has copyright protection. You can use the book for personal purpose. You should not sell, use, alter, distribute, quote, take excerpts or paraphrase in part of whole the material contained in this book without obtaining the permission of the author first.

Disclaimer Notice: You must take note that the information in this document is for casual reading and entertainment purpose only. We have made every attempt to provide accurate, up to date and reliable information. We do not express or imply guarantees of any kind. The person who read admit that the writer is not occupied in giving legal, financial, medical or other advice. We put this book content by sourcing various places. Please consult a licensed professional before you try any techniques shown in this book. By going through this document, the book lover comes to an agreement that under no situation is the author accountable for any forfeiture, direct or indirect, which they may incur because of the use of material contained in this document, including, but not limited to, - errors, omissions, or inaccuracies.

www.ingramcontent.com/pod-product-compliance
Lightning Source LLC
Chambersburg PA
CBHW061104070526
44579CB00011B/130